The Comfort Book

For <u>all</u> who hurt

by Lauri Withers

Bible verses in this book are quoted from one of the following translations:

Scripture taken from the NEW AMERICAN STANDARD BIBLE®, Copyright © 1960,1962, 1963,1968,1971,1972,1973,1975,1977,1995 by The Lockman Foundation. Used by permission.

THE HOLY BIBLE, NEW INTERNATIONAL VERSION®, NIV® Copyright © 1973, 1978, 1984, 2011 by Biblica, Inc.® Used by permission. All rights reserved worldwide.

Scripture taken from The Message. Copyright © 1993, 1994, 1995, 1996, 2000, 2001, 2002. Used by permission of NavPress Publishing Group.

The King James Version of The Holy Bible is available in the Public Domain.

Text and Illustrations Copyright © 2009-2015 by Lauri Withers

All rights reserved. This book is protected under the copyright laws of the United States of America. This book may not be copied or reprinted for commercial gain or profit.

Hardback Book: ISBN 978-1-943523-08-5
Paperback Book: ISBN 978-1-943523-09-2
Kindle: ISBN 978-1-943523-10-8
ePub for Nook and iBooks: ISBN 978-1-943523-11-5

Published by Laurus Books

Printed in the United States of America

Laurus Books

Laurus Books is an imprint of:
THE LAURUS COMPANY
www.TheLaurusCompany.com

Dedication

To the glory and honor
of my Lord and Savior, Jesus Christ,
who graciously still parts "Red Seas" and
makes gardens bloom in the wilderness.

~ My Story ~

My childhood
was <u>not</u> a childhood.
Abandonment, terror, confusion and wanting
to die don't make for "warm memories" of growing up.
Somehow, <u>I</u> survived.
So did you.

Do you carry scars like me?
Scars on the inside that no one can see?

Evil is alive and well; raw, pure evil. Evil for the sake of evil. We can see it in the frightened eyes of abused children and traumatized adults all over the world. Those of us who have experienced trauma on <u>any</u> level, whether extreme or as a one-time terrifying event, know horror in a way that honestly defies description. It's often difficult to reach out for help in the first place, let alone obtain the almost constant support and encouragement survivors need.

I am a scar bearer.
You are a scar bearer.
There's another who is also a scar bearer; Jesus.
His scars are able to do something ours can't.
His scars can heal. His scars can impart life. His scars prove how much He loves us.

As I write this book, I am in the middle of my healing journey. I want to share with you some of the Bible verses that have brought me comfort, as well as some poetry and words to songs. I pray that these pages might bring you some hope and to remind you that you are not alone. Survivors are everywhere. God knows where each one of us is "hiding". He is on our side. *I wish you <u>His</u> peace.*

Nightsounds©

Poem by my special friend, Gennet Emery
Used by Permission

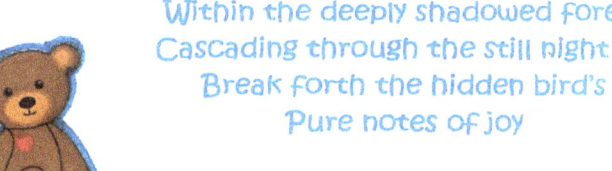

Within the deeply shadowed forest
Cascading through the still night air
Break forth the hidden bird's
Pure notes of joy

Although she does not even know
If dawn will ever come again
Or when
Yet on she sings
To welcome that sweet benison of light

In dark and lonely night travail of soul
O give my spirit grace to sing
Before the dawn

We are still alive... could this fact alone be a song in God's ears? As He listens intently to our weary prayers, when He hears our tearful sigh or sob, when He feels us take yet one more breath instead of committing suicide ~ does He hear the music of life that still beats in our hearts?

Sometimes, I surprise myself and I find I am able to sing praises to God, and at other times, my hands grip the pews in my church as I struggle to even stand and breathe. I believe the more we heal, the more we will sing songs of joy to our Heavenly Father. But I can't help but wonder if simply choosing to live is a source of music to our Lord...

> In the same way, the Spirit helps us in our weakness. We do not know what we ought to pray for, but the Spirit himself intercedes for us with groans that words cannot express.
>
> Romans 8:26 (NIV)

There have been many times when all I could manage to pray in a moment of desperation was one precious word:

"Jesus!"

And I knew He understood...

Jesus

> *"Do not fear, for I have redeemed you; I have called you by name you are mine."*
>
> Isaiah 43:1b (NASB)

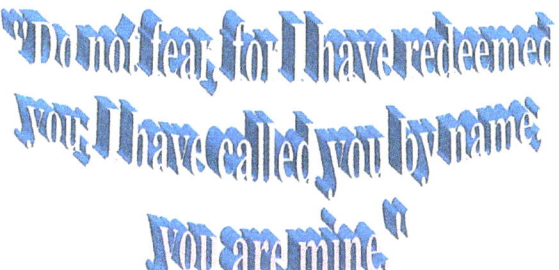

Do you have a hard time feeling like you <u>truly belong</u> to anyone? That you are extra special to at least one person? As an abuse survivor, I felt alone and unwanted from my earliest memories. As a child, I never felt special to anyone. Can you relate?

I am reminded of a statement made by a child who was asked, "How can you tell when somebody loves you?" He answered, "By the way your name sounds in their mouth." How simply profound! I wonder how lovingly God says the names of His treasured children? Can you imagine Him gently calling your name because He knows immediately when you are afraid? Or can you picture Him holding you close and whispering His soothing reminder, "You are Mine"? He knows like no other, how much comfort you need. He who redeemed you has plans for you that involve healing and wholeness. His arms are open wide, and your name rolls beautifully off His tongue. Even if you don't sense it yet, <u>you do belong</u>. You are redeemed. You are intimately known and the Spirit is aware of each of your emotions at any given time.

You belong to God and no one can take your inheritance from you.

> A bruised reed He will not break and a dimly burning wick He will not extinguish; He will faithfully bring forth justice.
>
> Isaiah 42:3 (NASB)

Our loving God knows how fragile we are as abuse survivors. He knows we are bruised. He knows whatever flame might have kept us going for a while might be down to a faint spark. This comforting verse shows us how gentle and protective God is. He's not out to destroy us or punish us as we might have been programmed to believe. Instead, when I read this verse, I feel that Christ is very near to nurture His bruised reed and breathe life back into what little spark we might have left. Not only that ~ but it also adds that He will bring forth justice! Some day, some time, those who tormented us will have to stand <u>**face to face with God Almighty**</u> and answer for what they did to His precious child. But in the meantime, we can rest in the knowledge that Jesus is gently tending to His wounded little one, bringing the deep healing that only He can give.

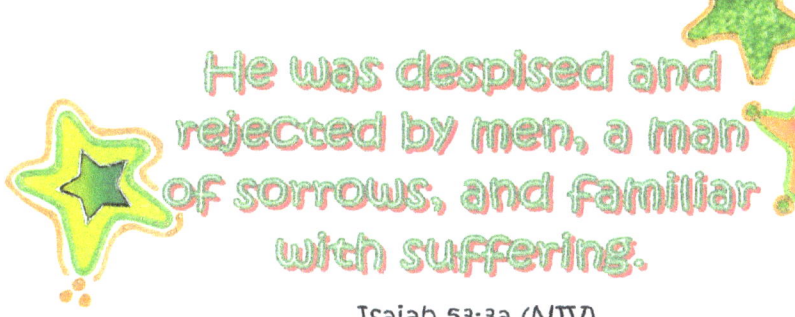

He was despised and rejected by men, a man of sorrows, and familiar with suffering.

Isaiah 53:3a (NIV)

If all you can do at this moment is cry out, "Jesus" or "God, help", know that He is right there. The One who has suffered most will not abandon you for a split second: *"Never will I leave you; never will I forsake you" (Heb. 13:5b NIV).* This is a promise we can cling to in our darkest moments.

Jesus can sincerely empathize with your grief because *He experienced profound sorrow first hand.* When He chose to live among us as God in the flesh, He allowed Himself to be exposed to the harsh realities that can afflict human beings. Isaiah says our Savior was a man of sorrows and "familiar" with suffering. It doesn't sound like He suffered from time to time; instead, it sounds like He suffered often. Christ also faced rejection ~ not just by strangers but by members of *His own earthly family:* "When his family heard about this, they went to take charge of him, for they said, 'he is out of his mind' " (Mark 3:21 NIV). John 7:5 (NIV) adds, "For even his own brothers did not believe in him." Feel familiar? Have you been rejected or despised by family members or friends for openly acknowledging your abuse / trauma? Jesus has been right where you are, and He hurts with you. The One who can relate most to your heartache is near ~ so very near.

When you pass through the waters, I will be with you; and through the rivers, they will not overflow you.

Isaiah 43:2 (NASB)

Years ago, a special friend of mine showed me a poem from her mother's diary, who had immigrated to Canada from Germany just before Hitler came to power. The words from the following poem are inspiring, speaking of God's faithfulness in our darkest storms. Neither my friend nor I are sure what the actual title is or even who authored it ~ it could be that her mother, Helen (Zimmerman) Clark penned it, or someone I am not able to credit. Although uncertain of the author, I hope you find some comfort in these words.

However Deep the Waters
(Author Unknown)

Is there any soul discouraged, as it journeys on its way,
Does there seem to be more darkness than there is of sunny day?
Oh it's hard to learn the lesson as we pass beneath the rod
That the sunshine and the shadow serve alike the will of God.
But there comes a word of promise, like the promise in the bow,
That however deep the waters, they will never overflow.

When the flesh is worn and weary and the spirit is depressed,
And temptations sweep upon it like a storm on ocean's breast.
There's a haven ever open for the tempest driven bird
There's a shelter for the tempted in the promise of the Word.
For the standard of the Spirit shall be raised against the foe,
That however deep the waters, they shall never overflow.

When a sorrow comes upon you that no other soul can share
And it seems to be too heavy for a human heart to bear,
There is One who's grace can comfort if you'll give Him an abode,
There's a Burden Bearer ready if you'll trust Him with your load,
For the precious promise reaches to the depths of human woe,
That however deep the waters, they shall never overflow.

When the sands of life are ebbing and I reach its Jordan shore,
And I see its waters rising and I hear its billows roar,
I will give my hand to Jesus, in His bosom I will hide
And twill only be a moment till I reach the other side.
And it's then the fullest meaning of the promise I shall know
That however deep the waters, they shall never overflow.

> **I will never desert you, nor will I ever forsake you.**
>
> Hebrews 13:5b (NASB)

Most abuse / trauma survivors particularly fear rejection and abandonment, especially if as children, they were wounded by their parents or any adult guardian they needed and depended on.

> Hebrews 13:5 is a reassuring promise from our faithful Savior. He will never desert us. He will never forsake us. He knows this kind of anguish. The Father could not be with Jesus as He bore our sins. He could not comfort His Son as He died an agonizing death. God is so utterly holy, He cannot in any way tolerate the presence of sin. Jesus cried out, "My God, my God, why have you forsaken me?" (Matt. 27:46). What a heart-wrenching scene.

You and I have experienced heart-wrenching events as well.

Because Christ conquered evil, He can carry all our horrors, no matter how overwhelming they are. He's been there. He's seen it all. And He made a way for us to walk with Him through the "valley of the shadow of death". That's you and that's me, walking with our God who will forever walk with us.

I Will Change Your Name
By DJ Butler ©

I will change your name,
You shall no longer be called
wounded, outcast, lonely or afraid.

I will change your name,
Your new name shall be:
Confidence, Joyfulness, Overcoming-one,
Faithfulness, Friend of God,
One Who Seeks My Face.

Hopefully the words of this song will bring you some comfort as it has to me.

There are several instances in the Bible where God changed people's names along with their purposes; for example, Abram became Abraham, Sarai became Sarah, Jacob became Israel, Simon became Peter, and Saul became Paul. And surprisingly, tucked into a verse in Revelation 2:17, Jesus tells us, *"He who has an ear, let him hear what the Spirit says to the churches. To him who overcomes, to him I will give some of the hidden manna, and I will give him a* **white stone, and a new name written on the stone** *which no one knows but he who receives it."*

A new name ~ think on that... One day, Christ Himself will place in your hand a white stone with your new name on it – and only you and He will know it. I wonder if it's the name He already calls us in our heart even now ~ His very special name, chosen just for you.

Copyright: © 1987 MERCY/VINEYARD PUBLISHING
(ASCAP) "All Rights Reserved. Used By Permission"

> **For my mother and my father have forsaken me, but the Lord will take me up.**
>
> Psalms 27:10 (NASB)

Many survivors were abused by one or both of their parents or main caretaker/s. The ones we needed so desperately to love and nurture us, feed and clothe us, protect us from evil, turned on us. *"Can a mother forget the baby at her breast and have no compassion on the child she has borne? Though she may forget, I will not forget you!" (Isaiah 49:15 NIV).* Having been rejected by the one I trusted and needed most has literally shaken me to my core. The grief I have experienced runs deep and can be triggered by the smallest of things... When I first read these passages in the Bible, I was both amazed and comforted. I was amazed that they were in scripture in the first place (making me aware that I am not the only one who has been forsaken by a parent), but then also comforted by the promise that God is with me -- never forgetting about me and always taking care of me. I believe God completely understands the depth of pain felt by anyone who has been abused or traumatized. As I heal, I am finding God is my safe parent -- the Mom and Dad I have always longed for. I am learning to trust His love more and more each day. If my mom doesn't want to hold and comfort me, I know now that Jesus does. I pray you too will find Him as your refuge of safety.

I will not forget you.

Cast all your anxiety on Him because He cares for you.

1 Peter 5:7b NIV)

Jesus cares so much for you. He always will. He always has ~ even as you survived each and every abusive moment. He couldn't leave your side. He loved you too much to leave you... He cares for you more than you can fathom. Tell him how you feel and let out your tears. His arms are safe and He will hold you.

And lo, I am with you always, even to the end of the age.
Matthew 28:20b (NASB)

God is and always has been with us. He is with you right now, whether you are relishing a moment of peace, or if you are in the middle of a terrifying storm. Did you know there is no place we can go that we are beyond His life saving reach? *"Where can I go from your Spirit? Or where can I flee from your presence? If I ascend to heaven, You are there. If I make my bed in Sheol, behold, You are there... when I awake, I am still with You" (Psalm 139:7-8, 18b).*

At this present moment, I am really hurting. So I offer up my prayer to Him: "Lord, my grief is so heavy. Please hold me in your lap so I can rest my weary head against your safe chest. Please wrap your protective arms around me. Hold me closer than close. Don't let go! I was never held enough, so don't ever put me down." Amen.

You may experience times when God "seems" far away – maybe because your terror / pain is off the charts, or you might feel you aren't "doing things quite right" to help God "speed up" your recovery. Whatever your situation, our faithful God is all around you. And if you should fall asleep reading this, keep in mind, when you wake up, you will still be with Him.

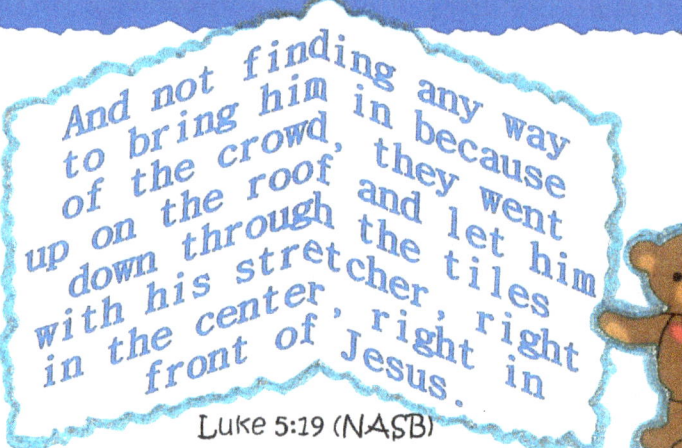

> And not finding any way to bring him in because of the crowd, they went up on the roof and let him down through the tiles with his stretcher, right in the center, right in front of Jesus.
>
> Luke 5:19 (NASB)

Do you have an established "support team" of trusted people to help encourage you as you walk through your healing process? If not, it is crucial as abuse / trauma survivors to develop a "support team" to turn to when a crisis hits. (If you don't have a support system available yet, ask your therapist to help you in this area). All of us need help from time to time. None of us can make it through life alone – especially if we are taking the courageous step of embarking on a significant healing journey. Sometimes though, it's hard to ask for help, especially if we are in immense pain and feel we have asked for help more than should be "allowed."

The man in this passage needed help. He was paralyzed and could not go to Jesus on his own. Some men chose to carry him on his stretcher to the house where Jesus was speaking so he might be healed (read Luke 5:18-26 for the rest of the story). Aren't we trauma survivors also "paralyzed", but in emotional ways? Our injuries may not show up as noticeable as a cast on a broken leg or as in someone battling a devastating disease. However, emotional wounds are just as painful and debilitating. Somehow, we've convinced ourselves that its "acceptable" to ask for help for physical needs, but not for deep emotional wounds that continue to ache as we heal.

My support team has carried me several times to Jesus' feet. My pain can become so "paralyzing" I can't think straight. So my faithful "stretcher carriers" bring me before our Lord through hugs, prayer, validating my feelings, and lots of love. Right now I wonder; who is "blessed" more by what Christ does in our midst ~ me, or my "Jesus-with-skin-on-family"?

If we are faithless, He remains faithful; for He cannot deny Himself.

2 Timothy 2:13 (NASB)

I don't know about you, but there are times when I really struggle with believing God's promises. I know in my "head" **He cannot break His word or promises**. However, I often battle such intense terror or pain, my "heart" starts doubting if His words are actually meant *for me!* I frequently question my sanity, which only deepens my pain. Post Traumatic Stress (and its accompanying symptoms) is complex enough – let alone wondering if I am "crazy" in a way that can't be helped! Do you ever feel this desperate? It's a scary place to be. I have to be re-assured over and over by patient friends that God isn't finished with me yet and that He will **remain faithful**. As I write this, I am in the middle of a tsunami size storm. I am weak, doubtful and exhausted. In the middle of my hell, I sensed the Holy Spirit quietly reminding me yesterday, "**I will not leave you as orphans;** I will come to you." (John 14:18 NASB). And you know what? He did. He came to me through two friends and my counselor. He wrapped His hope around me through them. Yes, I'm still shaky today, but God came to me. *He came to me!*

IMPORTANT: If you are in a desperate place, call someone or go to your next-door neighbor. DO NOT TAKE YOUR LIFE ~ YOU MATTER! The person you reach out to will be so glad you asked for their help. Let God come to your rescue through your friends or therapist. You are worth it.

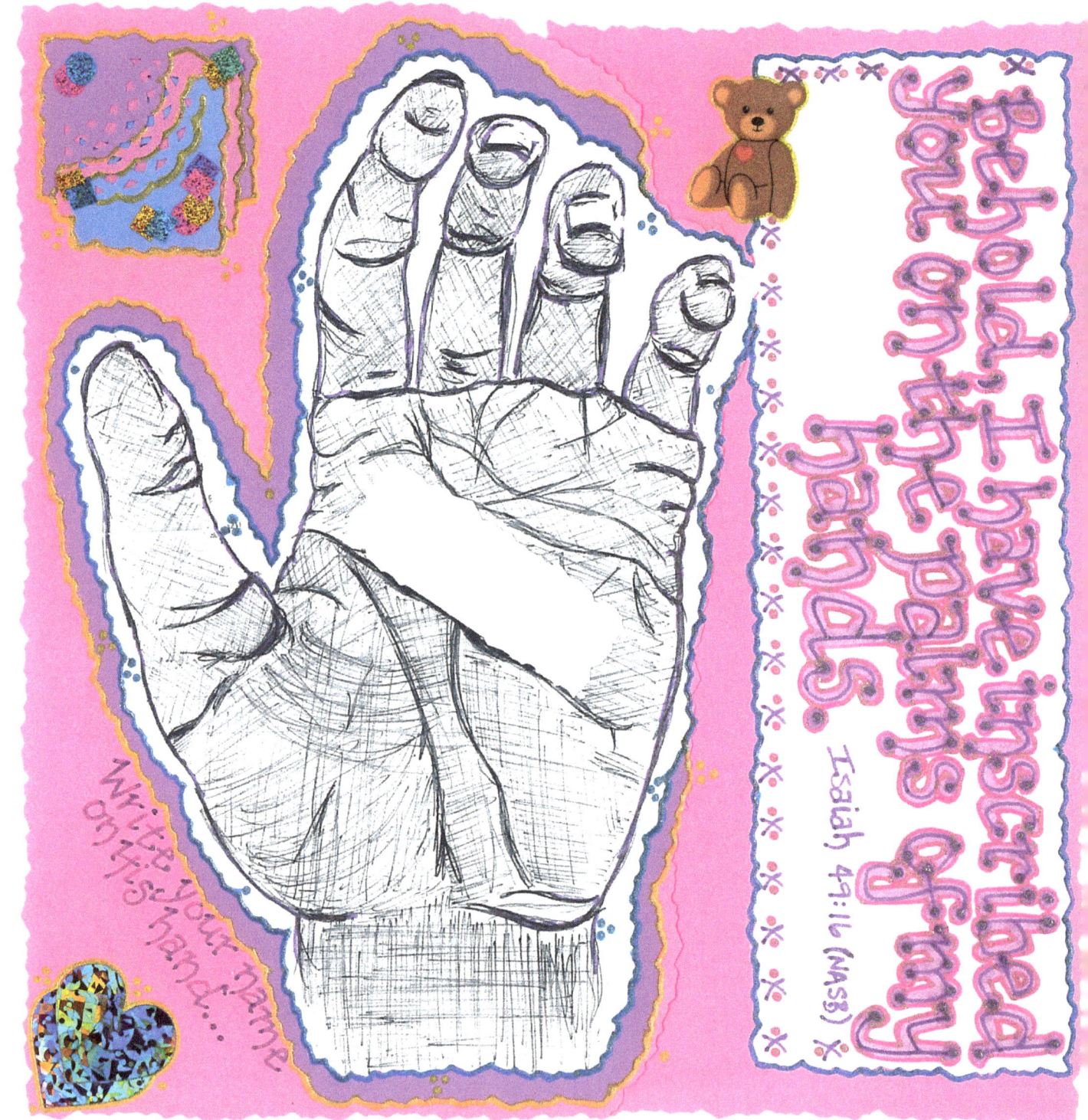

Proverbs 18:24b (NASB)

If you find yourself alone or with few allies who support you, keep in mind, you have a friend who sticks

"...closer than a brother".

God will never give up on you. He will walk with you every step of the way as you heal. Family or friends may walk away, but this Faithful Friend will stay close beside you.

I will not leave you as orphans; I will come to you.

John 14:18 (NIV)

Many of us know what it is like to be orphaned. Perhaps death, divorce or abandonment took your beloved parents / caretakers from you. Your world turned upside down and nothing was ever the same.

Some of us though, may feel "orphaned" because we were the children of adults that abused and betrayed. The faces we looked to for love and protection, food and shelter, forced us into a life of dark secrets. We too lived in an upside down world where nothing was safe or certain.

Facing our past is important and worth all of our efforts to heal. But it can also be painful at times. We may agonize because "instant cures" don't exist. We might even be angry or disappointed with God and His "one-step-at-a-time" healing method. God's compassion is big enough to handle our anger. His love runs far deeper than our emotions. In the middle of our despairing cries, He promises, *"I will come to you."* And He does. Christ is the One who seeks and saves. He loves His treasured children, His little ones (yes, you and me). He will never orphan, abuse, or abandon. Never.

May those of us who have become orphans in one way or another, find our loving parent and safe home in the heart of God.

The Lord is close...

The Lord is close to the brokenhearted and saves those who are crushed in spirit.

Psalm 34:18 (NIV)

Here are some protective words to wrap around yourself. Just like a soft, warm blanket, envelop yourself in the comfort of these words. Jesus is so near, holding you, collecting your tears and taking to heart the speechless language of your despair. There is no language He doesn't understand ~ even the sighs of silence.

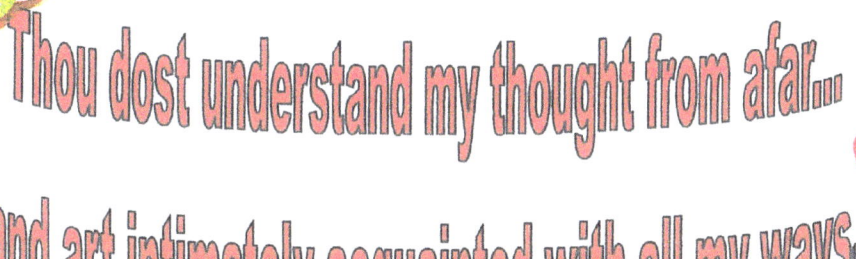

Thou dost understand my thought from afar...

and art intimately acquainted with all my ways

Psalm 139:2b & 3b (NASB)

Like a loving parent who knows exactly why their child is afraid of the dark, God understands all of our ways. Nothing we do to hide or cope surprises Him. He can see how we will react "from afar" before we even know what's around the corner. So the next time you find yourself crouching in the tightest corner of your closet, hang onto the truth that Jesus understands. If you find you still can't face the overwhelming world outside your home yet, realize that Jesus is intimately acquainted with your feelings.

He knows you well. You are understood as you shake alone in your darkness. The God of the universe is right beside you.

Jesus Wept.

John 11:35 (NASB)

John 11 says that Jesus was "deeply moved and troubled" by Mary and Martha's grief over the death of their brother, Lazarus. In fact, He was so affected that He didn't just cry, "*He wept.*" This same Jesus feels your heartache and catches your tears.

God knows exactly how we feel. He has *always been with us* and perhaps even experienced our abuse as we endured it *(I will never leave you or forsake you; Hebrews 13:5)*. I have often found myself asking Jesus ***"why?"*** He didn't intervene and rescue me from my very real hell. Does it all come down to the fact that He gave human beings the gift of "free will"? This gift grants all of us the freedom to choose good or evil, love or hatred, and whether or not we want to be in personal relationship with God. Free will is part of our humanity. We get to decide for ourselves how we want to live and if we want to love.

As you and I are well aware, some people choose to do evil and hurt us in horrific ways. Others choose to love and want to be our friends and walk with us as we heal.

This brings me back to Jesus, the one who weeps with us, the one who deeply loves us, the one who understands us most because He was in our hell with us. He kept us alive for something greater than what we survived. You are not alone in your pain. He is right there weeping with you.

Mended Heart©
1992 ~ By KR ~ to LM
Used by permission

Your story's starting to unfold,
It's led you down a rocky road
Weighted down by years of fear,
The path has led you here,
Cold and alone.

I know you've struggled for so long,
And the battle has left you far from strong,
But it's only when you are weak,
That the Father's love can speak,
To your broken heart.

Chorus:
He wants to offer you, life in abundance,
If you give Him your broken heart, He'll mend it in time.
His promise lives in you, if you'll allow Him to,
He'll make of your life a testament of His grace and love.

Bridge:

Only love can take the pain away,
Healing wounds worn raw with time,
Bringing hope where there was emptiness,
Changing the storyline…

The seed of understanding grows,
You're learning all you need to know,
A new chapter will unfold
Written on a mended heart ~
Filled with hope.

Lord, please make of my life a testament of your grace and love.
Amen

I Sing You©
By LM

(V1)

Back then in the darkness,
You held him to your heart,
Unaware ~ You were there…

Trusted hands she reached for,
Betrayed her to their schemes,
Unaware ~ You were there…

> Little ones so frightened didn't see,
> Your hands were wrapped around them as their shield;

Chorus:
I sing You to the hurting,
I sing You to the lost,
I sing You to the orphaned,
I sing You, our healing God.
> *I sing You to the widowed,*
> *Who cries prayers beneath your stars,*
> *I sing You, My Lord Jesus ~*
> *Who alone can heal hearts.*

(V2)

In the dust of a village,
They hide from nightly raids -
Unaware ~You are there…

Huddled near the shooting,
And the bombs that light dark skies,
Unaware ~ You are there…

> I pray Your name for those in deep despair,
> So they will know You hear their fragile prayers;

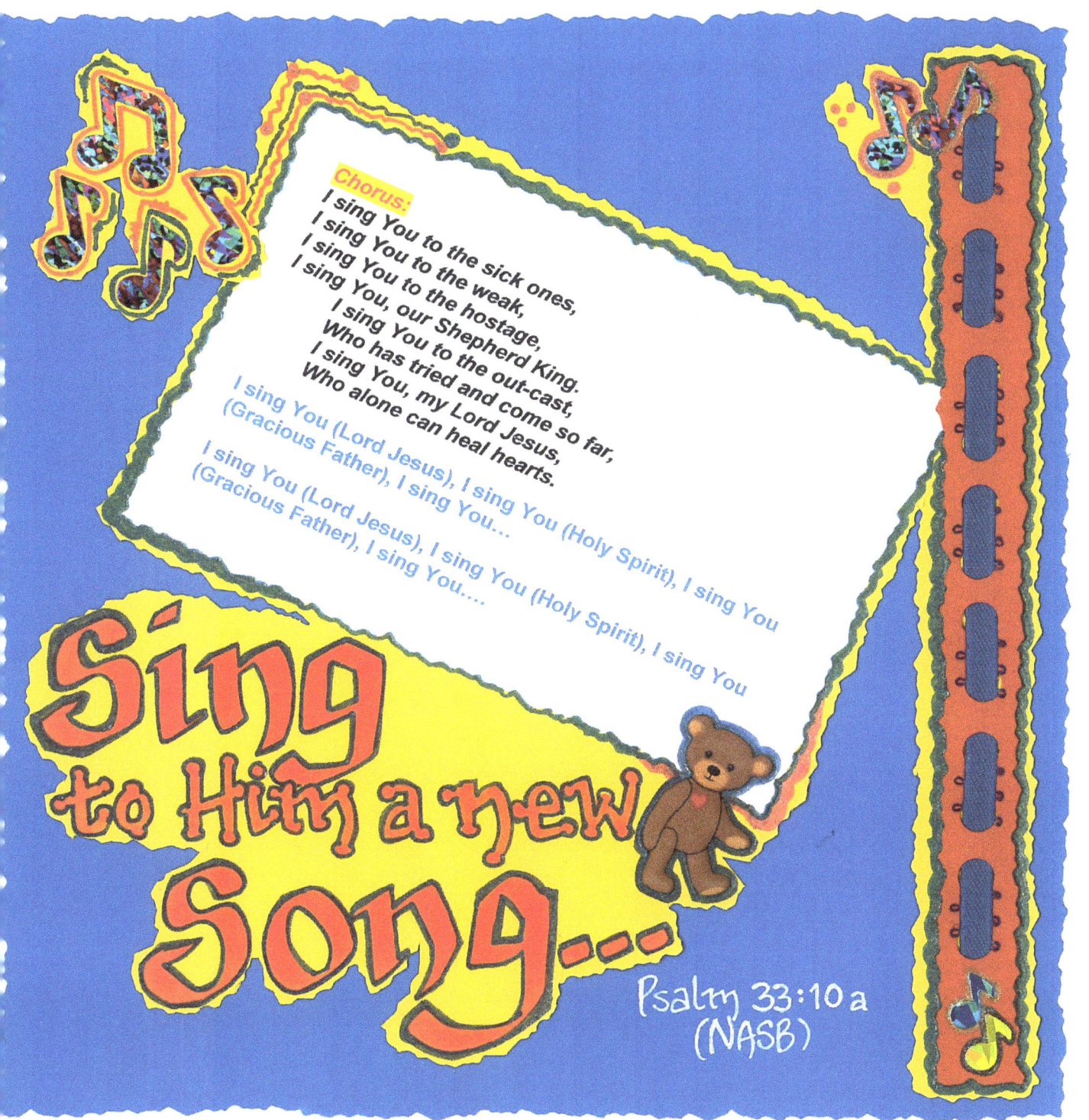

> The LORD your God is in your midst,
> A Victorious warrior.
> He will exult over you with joy,
> He will be quiet in His love,
> He will rejoice over you with shouts of joy.
>
> Zephaniah 3:17 NASB

Just think ~ *our God rejoices over you.* Were you delighted in as a child? Were you respected and appreciated as a teen? Or, instead, were you ignored? Alone? Used?

As an adult, were you belittled? Attacked? Rejected by your spouse?

Your victorious warrior is in your midst. He always has been. If He hadn't been with you, things could be so much worse... You mattered to Him before you were even born. The Father has constantly delighted over you as His treasure even if no one else did.

You were and are Christ's precious lamb.
He is not finished rejoicing over you
with shouts of joy!

Psalm 23

1 The Lord is my shepherd, I shall not want.

2 He makes me lie down in green pastures; He leads me beside quiet waters.

3 He restores my soul; He guides me in the paths of righteousness for His name's sake.

4 Even though I walk through the valley of the shadow of death, I fear no evil, for You are with me; Your rod and Your staff, they comfort me.

5 You prepare a table before me in the presence of my enemies; You have anointed my head with oil; my cup overflows.

6 Surely goodness and lovingkindness will follow me all the days of my life, and I will dwell in the house of the Lord forever.

New American Standard Bible (NASB)

About The Author

Author Lauri Withers is a multi-talented and creative woman who is in team ministry with her pastor/teacher husband, Rich. Lauri accompanies him by leading worship with her guitar.

In her spare time, Lauri enjoys reading Christian fiction, cross stitching, scrapbooking, card making, and embarking on prayer drives with her husband through the beautiful Pacific Northwest.

They reside in Spokane, Washington, and are the proud parents of a Himalayan-Tabby-Persian cat named Percy.

www.ingramcontent.com/pod-product-compliance
Lightning Source LLC
Chambersburg PA
CBHW041437040426
42453CB00020B/2449